A

Woman

Being

A

Woman

Mya G. Wolf

Being a Woman

ISBN: 9798377459187

Contents

For my Mother and her Mother

Thank you for showing me what strong women look like

I love you both

I

Sweet Nothings

When I was a girl

The world felt infinite

As I got older

The sky started closing in on me

In high school, all I wanted was male approval

I wanted the boys to like me because that's what I saw on T.V

So, when they pressured me into giving them what they wanted

I almost always caved

But since I was a girl, all that left me with was shame

Those boys would be praised, even though they were halfway to blame

I was called a slut

But they could walk away without having to carry my burdens

The crippling weight of being a woman

My teenage days were plagued with

Too tight push-up bras

Wires digging in my skin

Burnt hair and

Razor bumps on my shins

Flower scented tampons

Hidden in my backpack

Never ending dress codes

So we didn't distract

The gym coach

Boys will be boys

And I tried to be their cool girl

That's what I thought I was supposed to be

I spent too much of my adolescence trying to be good for men.

As a girl, I was failed because I was told that if a boy picks on you- he likes you. I was failed because I grew up watching movies that told me boys were what made me valuable. In order to be a princess, I needed a man. I let so many boys treat me like shit because I was trying to become the queen I so desperately wanted to be.

Our graves were dug for us

The moment we were labeled "female"

We must conjure up the strength

To dig through the dirt

And reclaim our rightful crown

I didn't realize that in order to become a Queen

I had to love myself first

I was just the girl you came to when you were lonely. You couldn't stand being alone. I was always on call for you, wanting to prove that I was worthy. I was "different" than the other girls. A gem you always kept hidden. You kept me hanging by a thread- feeding me sweet nothings so I would never leave. I never met your friends. You never posted pictures of me.

I was the thing you used when you were lonely.

I liked being your dumping ground

Your empty words were like kisses to my
bruised self-confidence

My heart aches for the girl I was

I wish I could go back in time

And be her knight in shining armor

White dresses stained red

This is what unites us as women

We can bathe in bleach

But we never feel the same again

Being a daughter is helping with dinner while your brother plays video games. Being a daughter is healing your mother's trauma while also healing your own. Being a daughter is forgiving your father... over and over again.

Being a daughter is the lifelong burden of carrying the heavy weight dumped onto to you by your elders.

Like clothes that fit too big.

Strip me of all that makes me a woman

So that I can finally exist in peace

Late at night I cry to the full moon

She shines in all her glory

And I ask her

"Why can't I shine as bright as you?"

She chuckles and says

"Little one, there are days I travel through that dark void too"

Teary eyed girl

Fall into my embrace

Weep until you are new again

Put down your sword

You can't save anyone

Until you save yourself

You told me I was your sunshine

But when I didn't shine the way you wanted

The flowers stopped growing

And the clouds turned grey

Your darkness strangled my light

You didn't love me

You just didn't want me to leave

I was easily replaceable

But you found my fragile wings so beautiful

You wouldn't dare set me free

It didn't matter if I was happy

As long as I was yours

You grasped on so tight

I could barely breathe

Your selfish "love" nearly *killed me*

He acted like a child disguised as a man

Throwing a tantrum

Because I wasn't being what he wanted me to be

I was becoming something loud

When he wanted me to stay silent

I was becoming my own

When he wanted me to be his forever

And he couldn't stand the sight of it

I am not that sad girl you once knew

You broke her

And when I left you

I got to put myself back together

Piece by piece

So differently than the way you once saw me

I am everything you never wanted me to be

Don't blame me for these graves you've conjured

Being a strong woman is not a sin

I remember sitting in the car with you

Picturing myself with somebody else

I wonder if you were doing the same

Neither of us wanting to admit

That it was the end

Growing up, we take our friendships for granted. You don't realize how precious female friendships are until you've completely grown apart. Nothing hurts more than drifting away from the women you loved most.

Please don't look so closely at me

Don't ask me how I am really doing

I would tell you that I hate the walls you built

I hate that you are protecting yourself from me

Please let me in

Please show me what you've been so desperately
hiding

I never felt lonelier than the night of your birthday party. You were drunk with your friends, laughing and telling me all of the things you said behind my back. The next morning you didn't even remember what you had said. You opened my gift- I wrapped it up perfectly. It was filled with our greatest memories.

I cried myself to sleep that night knowing our best days were behind us.

Losing a best friend feels like losing a piece of your soul

I've been trying to rip out the cord

you struck in me

Its claws run deep

I pull with my nails and my teeth

But the fantasy of what I wanted us to be

Keeps my mind from breaking free

I stare at myself and see both a little girl and woman staring back at me. The little girl can move mountains. She is fearless. The woman is always one step ahead. She moves with ease as I try to keep up. They both want to light the fire simmering within me.

Can I be what they need me to be?

Mascara runs down my cheeks in the bathroom as I get ready to go out. I wipe my face and force a smile. I reapply my makeup and leave my house wearing my pretty mask.

Being a woman, it is better to show up looking put together than to let anyone know that you are breaking on the inside.

There are days when I have to remind myself not to stare at my body so harshly. If I look for too long, I find nothing but skin and bone.

No more light and no more soul.

It is easy to objectify yourself

When you have been objectified your whole life

I have to remind myself to be gentle

My body has been through so much already

Being a woman comes with many burdens. We are given a list of imperfections that we must memorize and carry, distracting us from the fact that we created every single soul walking on this planet. Life would be non-existent without the body and spirit of a woman. And yet we must prove ourselves time and time again to entitled men- who should be on their hands and knees thanking us for the life we breathed into them.

Women are victims of a society that makes money off our self-hate

Why do women have to work so hard to feel good about themselves?

Our worthiness is not a privilege

Who took our worthiness away? Who made it
hard to love ourselves?

We should feel worthiness because we are alive

We should feel worthiness because we are *women*

It has been hardwired into our brains to look in the mirror and not be happy with what we see

II

Cracked Open

I hate feeling like the object of men's pleasure. A thing they like to look at. A thing they use to hear themselves speak.

I am not your audience

I don't want you to try and entertain me

I don't find you funny

When I walk down the street it is not for you

I am not free therapy

I don't want to hear how your wife isn't fun anymore after she had your babies

I know all you want to do is sleep with me

But I am not some toy you get to play with when you are horny

A woman's existence is not solely for men's
pleasure

To the men who degrade and sexualize us

To the men who use violence to control us

To the men who cheat and lie and manipulate

To the men who hate us and just want to fuck us

How dare you betray the pussy

that pushed you out into this world?

Being a woman

There are times I confuse kindness with
manipulation

I'd rather be ignored by a man on the street

Than smiled at by one

True heartbreak happens when a girl is forced
into womanhood too soon

We are told we "mature faster than boys"

But maybe our childhood was stolen from us too soon

Boys were blessed with the freedom of ignorance

While we lost our innocence

My girlhood was taken from me on the school bus,
where I was picked apart by the boys each day.
My body was never good enough for them; so I
begged my mom for pushup bras and straightened
my hair each morning at thirteen. These boys
would watch me with certainty, grab my ass and
thighs. I was called a slut if I received attention
from other guys. They talked about porn and they
taught me that being a woman was their fantasy
and my hell.

Sinking to my knees each night

I prayed to a God I hardly believed in

I begged him to send me a new body

I wanted to look like a woman

Because the boys were hungry

Circling me like sharks

Waiting for me to turn into something they could
eat

I can't even count the number of times a man has looked at me like I was his next meal. There is nothing more sickening than feeling like a piece of meat.

Smiling at the wrong man could get me killed

Pissing off the wrong man could get me killed

I'm tired

Dear Patriarchy

You are not allowed to have my body

You think the blood that paints my thighs is a turn off... but look at your video games and violent porn. Nobody bats an eye when a boy blows someone's head off online; but girls are still hiding tampons up their sleeves.

Violent men are seen as men

Violent women are seen as insane

     bitches

     witches

     hormonal

     dramatic

     etc....

I am tired of holding the weight of a million
unhealed men on my aching back

You should be afraid of a silenced woman

Centuries of being crushed by the heaviness of the patriarchy changes you

Men's rage has plagued our planet with war and greed and death...yet women are seen as the "emotional ones"

I survive off the idea that

One day

My rage will be witnessed by the men who
poisoned me with it in the first place

Learn to love your rage

And use it when they try to take our rights away

We have every right to feel angry

Men have let their rage rule for centuries

It's our time now

I can feel the pain of one thousand women before me

My ancestors watching me with their mouths sewn shut

Dreaming...but already in the stars

Can I be their king?

Can I slay this dragon?

How am I supposed to tell them that we are moving backwards?

Deeper into the belly of the beast

Women have to look out for men who could beat
or rape or kill them

Men have to look out for women who wear too
much makeup

Our dating experiences are not the same

Our red flags are not the same

Things I am Afraid of:

-going on a walk

-traveling alone

-going to the store

-parking lots

-pumping gas

-being home alone

-male authority figures

-one of my ex's

-movies with sexual assault scenes

-walking to my car at night

-public transportation

-etc....etc...etc....

Not a day goes by that I am afforded the luxury of feeling safe as a woman

Sometimes the fear gets so loud all I can do is lie
down and let it consume me

They tell us to get tattoos so we won't be as
appealing to sex traffickers

Like our own personal war paint

Protecting ourselves in such a permanent way

But what else can we do?

When no one else will step up to the plate

She did what she had to do to get on top

She lied and cheated

She stained her sword blood red

She let her rage overcome her

She did what any man would do...

And now they can't believe she is King

Don't underestimate a woman's power to turn
darkness into a beautiful thing

You place a woman in darkness

And she will become it

She will dance in it

She will devour it

Dear women,

It is time to stop smiling at the creepy men who feel entitled to our joy. Being nice to people who don't deserve it is exhausting. It's time to wear whatever the hell you want. Go get your tattoos and piercings. Let's reclaim the words bitches and sluts. Being a woman is a title within itself. We are natural born royalty.

They will try to call us villains, but we are becoming our own heroes and saving ourselves.

III

Queen Shit

I am realizing that everything deemed disgusting regarding my body is actually what makes me powerful.

Internalized misogyny is like a parasite we must purge from our bodies.

It is not our fault we were infected, but it is our job to heal.

Why do they want us

To fear our womanhood?

Maybe it is all a distraction

To make us forget our Godliness

I am no longer interested in trying to prove myself in a world that will never be satisfied.

Growth is sitting in a room full of people you've known your whole life

And feeling like a ghost of the person you used to be

My 20's may be lonely, but within this loneliness I am learning what brings me peace and what doesn't. In the morning my friend is the rising sun. In the evening I cry to the moon. She knows what it feels like to rest in the shadows. But the moon always reminds me that my time will come. And although I feel a little empty right now,

I know my time will come.

Don't tell me to get on my knees and pray

On Sundays I'll be in the forest

Talking to the trees

And dancing in the wind

Nature is my church

She is my God

And I will worship Her until the day I die

Look in the mirror and recognize that you share a bloodline with queens and soldiers and witches. We are descendants of powerful women.

Be proud of who you are.

I've watched my mother fight to break down the walls she built when her womanhood betrayed her.

This is what makes her strong.

I see myself reflected in the Earth

I see myself in the blooming flowers and the rotting trees

I see myself in the weeping clouds and golden autumn leaves

I see myself in the way she is treated

I see myself in the way she is underappreciated

I am learning to love myself unconditionally

This is an act of bravery in a society that demands
my self-loathing

I don't recognize the girl I see in the mirror

She intimidates me

And I'm really proud of that

I will become my own sun when the world feels
dark.

When I die, I hope my soul scatters across the night sky. I want my light to guide the women who come after me.

A woman is the rain and the sun that turns a seed into a beautiful thing

A woman is also the beautiful thing

A woman is the Earth that holds down the mighty tree

She is also the tree and its leaves

There is so much depth that comes with being a
woman

A woman can never be just one thing

Remember not to compete with your sisters

We are all losing against man

We can only win together

Even when your pictures aren't getting a lot of
likes, and your friends feel like strangers

Don't forget that you are Heaven in a human body

And you have the warmth of the sun in your belly

A woman's love can be felt for eternity

Make sure the people you surround yourself with
are worthy of that love

I found my King after remembering I was natural born royalty. He treats me like a Queen because I expect nothing less.

Never settle.

Sometimes I have to reflect and give thanks to my difficulties. Every heartbreak brought me greater love. Every time I hit rock bottom, I connected more deeply with myself. The darkness was my inspiration to look for the light.

Affirm this to yourself:

Every time I let go of something that no longer brings me joy, I grow into a more beautiful and confident version of myself.

Dear younger me,

Please keep singing even if you never feel heard. Keep climbing the trees higher and higher. And never stop telling the frogs on your window good night and sweet dreams. Please please please never stop dreaming. I know you stay up late watching the stars and wondering where the hell you came from. I hope you know you are the sun in human form.

Never stop shining.

To be a woman

Is a powerful thing

I hope all women find peace in being themselves. I hope all women receive the right to bodily autonomy. I hope all women one day feel safe in their bodies and out in the world. I hope all women remember their power.

I hope all women become their own knights in shining armor.

The end for now.

About the Author

Mya is a poet who dreams of inspiring and empowering her readers. Her poetry reflects her love of nature, her admiration of womanhood and her ability to turn her words into a work of art. At a young age Mya began reading and journaling religiously. She poured her thoughts into diaries, which later turned into poetry that she now shares with the world. When Mya was in high school she did her senior thesis on Feminism-thus sparking her love and interest in womanhood and the power of being a woman.

At the age of 21, Mya self-published her first poetry collection *Whispers of a Loud Soul* on Amazon. She sold her book in local bookstores in Louisiana (her home state) and read her poetry for multiple different poetry foundations.

Now, Mya has self-published her second poetry collection, *Being a Woman,* and is finishing her bachelor's degree in creative writing. She spends her free time walking along the river by her house, watching nostalgic movies and listening to music by badass female artist like MARINA, Stevie Nicks and Florence + The Machine.